P9-DNL-237

Books by Sarah Price

The Amish of Lancaster Series
#1 Fields of Corn
#2 Hills of Wheat
#3 Pastures of Faith
#4 Valley of Hope

The Amish of Ephrata Series
#1 The Tomato Patch
#2 The Quilting Bee

The Adventures of a Family Dog Series
#1 A Small Dog Named Peek-a-boo
#2 Peek-a-boo Runs Away
#3 Peek-a-boo's New Friends
#4 Peek-a-boo and Daisy Doodle

Other Books
Gypsy in Black
Postcards from Abby (with Ella Stewart)

Find Sarah Price on Facebook and Goodreads!
Learn about upcoming books, sequels, series, and contests!

The Quilting Bee:
The Amish of Ephrata

An Amish Novella on Morality

By
Sarah Price

Published by Price Publishing, LLC.
Morristown, New Jersey
2012

The Pennsylvania Dutch used in this manuscript is taken from the Pennsylvania Dutch Revised Dictionary (1991) by C. Richard Beam, Brookshire Publications, Inc. in Lancaster, PA.

Contact the author on Facebook at
http://www.facebook.com/fansofsarahprice or
visit her Web Blog at http://sarahpriceauthor.wordpress.com.

Price Publishing, LLC.
Morristown, NJ
http://www.pricepublishing.org

Dedicated to anyone who has ever experienced bullying, whether in person or on the Internet. It is my wish that people will read this book and recognize that false accusations, lies, and general bad will against others are clearly not Christian behavior.

This novella is dedicated to all of my friends and readers on Facebook, especially those from the Whoopie Pie Book Club Group, who provided greatly appreciated moral support when it was needed.

Chapter One

After a long summer, Priscilla Smucker was looking forward to the upcoming autumn. Cooler weather and shorter days meant that the apple trees would soon produce ripe, juicy fruit, perfect for making applesauce with her mamm. She loved to ride in their buggy with her mamm to the local market and bring home bountiful bushels of freshly picked apples. They would spend the day lovingly peeling them, coring them, cooking them, smashing them, and canning them. Afterwards, a hundred clear colored pint jars would line the shelves in mamm's pantry, just waiting for the winter months, when they would be at their best. The creamy gold color of the applesauce would contrast nicely on the shelves next to the dozens of canned red beets and chow-chow that they had already canned during July and August.

A cool breeze brushed against her face and Priscilla lifted her chin as she turned to face it. She shut her dark eyes and breathed in the crisp air. It was almost as if she could taste autumn in the air. When she opened her eyes, she looked around at the remnants of her garden that was already withering and brown. Yes, she loved autumn and making applesauce. Yet, she knew that this year, the applesauce canning wasn't what really excited her so much.

For the past few months, she had been courting Stephen Esh. He was as constant as milking cows...always there to pick her up and take her home from the Sunday singings. There was, indeed, no doubt that Stephen Esh had something a little more serious on his mind than just short buggy rides and occasional volley ball games with the other youths. And the thought that, mayhaps, her first come-calling friend would be her last certainly did not upset Priscilla the least.

She smiled as she thought about the handsome man that she secretly considered her beau.

Oh, how she enjoyed his company! She loved hearing his laughter and listening to his stories. He was older than her and already well-established in the community. While he still lived at home with his daed and mamm, he also had his own farm. Everyone thought quite a lot of Stephen Esh but he never once let that get to his head. He was modest about how hard he worked, helping his daed during the mornings and working his own farm in the late afternoons.

And he was wise. She loved when he gave her advice. Despite their age difference, he was never condescending. Instead, he would listen to her and think before he spoke. When he did speak, he grounded his words with the Scripture. He explained things to her, his voice soft and gentle. She always felt that he truly had her best interests at heart.

Priscilla stared at her dying garden. It had been a lovely season with wonderful, tasty vegetables. She would miss working in the garden, feeling the soil beneath her fingers, and smelling the beautiful scent of fresh tomatoes and zucchini and squash. But she knew that it wouldn't be long before she would be rebuilding the garden for the next season, perhaps her last one living at her parents' farm.

The thought made her blush. Just recently, Stephen had begun to tell her that he was fixing up the farmhouse. He even drove her by it one afternoon before the Sunday singing. They hadn't gotten out of the buggy to go explore the empty house. That would have been improper, for sure and certain. But he had pointed out the different locations such as the kitchen window, the canning room door, and corner of the house with the sitting room.

There was a distant look on his face as he stared at the house, quiet for just a few moments. She could tell that he was thinking hard about something and she gave him that time for reflection. Watching him, she noticed the straight line of his cheekbone and the firm tilt of his chin. He was such a hard worker and so determined to do well for his family, community, and church. His eyes seemed to travel across the farmland and she knew that he was taking in the commitment he had made to the land. She wondered whether he was excited or fearful of that prospect.

The answer was clear when he turned his head to look at her and he smiled. "Ja," he had said. "That's my future home."

That, too, had made her blush. They had only been courting for four months. While she knew that was enough time for some couples, she also knew that she wasn't quite seventeen yet and certainly not ready to make a commitment. She needed more time but, since Stephen never mentioned anything about baptism or marriage, she tried not to presume that he was hinting about it, either.

Leave it to her Mamm to take matters into her own hands, she thought. Mamm had suggested that they start thinking about making a quilt for Priscilla's hope chest. Her family had given it to her on her sixteenth birthday, a gift that her father had made with her brothers when she was busy in the house helping Mamm. Now, Mamm was hinting that they start thinking about filling it with household items that Priscilla would need for when she finally got married.

And that was what Priscilla was most excited about:

attending a quilting bee. In the autumn and winter, many of the families with young unmarried daughters had quilting bees. It was a time for the community to come together, to contribute to the making of the quilt that would, one day, cover the marriage bed. Quilting bees were a time for women to engage in fellowship, sharing stories and recipes, reminiscing about their own lives, and providing good advice for the young women. She hadn't been to many of them. Only three last year. But she hoped that they would be invited to a few this winter.

Whenever the women gathered for canning or baking, Priscilla tried to be there. She loved being around them. She found the older women to be interesting and lively with their sparkling eyes and warm laughter. She absorbed their energy for life as much as she could, trying to remember everything that they had said.

Afterwards, she would hurry to her room and eagerly write down the different things that they had shared with her. Recipes for making cheese, pickling beets, smoking beef, and canning meatballs were among her favorites. Her Mamm always laughed at her, reminding Priscilla to add all of the different recipes that they had made together over the years, lest she forget. Priscilla would just smile, too embarrassed to tell her mamm that those recipes were the first ones in her collection.

"Priscilla!" someone called from the porch.

She looked up, surprised to see her brother, Jonas, standing on the edge of the porch, waving his arm toward her. "Mamm says to come in now," he yelled.

With a quick glance back at the garden, she turned and hurried back to the farmhouse. Certainly it was getting close to

10

suppertime and Mamm needed her help with preparing the food and setting the table. What she couldn't understand was why Jonas was already in the house and not helping Daed with the evening chores in the dairy barn.

The screen door slammed behind her as she walked into the canning room. It was a large room off the kitchen, the place where she would work alongside her mamm during the late summer and early autumn months for canning vegetables, fruits, and meats. It always had a fresh smell to it and was one of her favorite rooms in the house.

Her brother was standing by the brick fireplace, fiddling around with the large cast iron pot that would cook the apples. He looked up when Priscilla walked into the room. "Mamm says I'm to take you for apples tomorrow," he said.

"Really?" Priscilla answered, turning her head to look toward the kitchen. Every year, Mamm took Priscilla to the market for the apples. It was a special time of year for the two of them, especially since Priscilla's older sisters had left the farm so many years ago. The bond that she had with her mamm was deeper than most daughters' had with their mamm, mostly because they spent so much time together. So, this was news indeed, for Mamm had never asked one of the boys or Daed to take her. So this news that Jonas had been recruited to accompany Priscilla surprised her. "Is she not feeling well then?"

Jonas shrugged. "Looks right as rain to me, I reckon," he said casually before kneeling down to sweep out the ashes from the fire pit beneath the pot. "There! That's should be all set for tomorrow." He wiped his hands on his pants as he stood up. "Best go back out to see if daed needs my help with the cows," he said before disappearing out the door.

Priscilla hurried into the kitchen and saw that Mamm was already preparing the evening meal. She was moving with lightning speed around the kitchen, her hands pulling down dishes and bowls from the cabinets. Priscilla walked toward her and reached out to take the plates in order to set the table. They moved in silence, each one knowing exactly what to do in order to get the table ready for supper.

Supper was a light meal in the Smucker household. Bread, chow-chow, pickled cabbage, cheese, and any other leftovers from the earlier meal were served most often. Sometimes Mamm made cup cheese and served it with pretzels, always a favorite of Priscilla and her brothers. But tonight, it was more simple fare.

"Jonas said he's to take me for apples tomorrow?" Priscilla asked hesitantly, "Any particular reason for that?"

Her mamm nodded. "Ja," she said. "Have to watch the *kinner* for Elsie."

This was news for Priscilla. It was Saturday and her older sister, Elsie, was always home on Saturdays. "Elsie OK?"

Her mamm smiled. "Just tired out these days," she said softly. "Feeling a bit poorly and needs some rest after being at market yesterday and today."

Priscilla smiled and asked no more questions. She didn't need to for it was clear that her older sister was expecting again. This would be her fourth baby, a great addition to Elsie's growing family, which included Katie, Ben, and Ruth Ann. There was nothing Priscilla enjoyed more than seeing the joy in her family when a new member was born. She was truly looking forward to the upcoming autumn and winter months now.

12

"Looks like it might rain tomorrow," Daed said as he entered the kitchen. He smiled at Priscilla as he walked past her to wash his hands in the sink. "Hear you're going to be making applesauce tomorrow, ja?"

Priscilla nodded. "150 quarts again this year, right Mamm?"

"That's awfully ambitious," Mamm said teasingly as she started setting the bowls of food onto the table.

Once everyone was seated, Daed bent his head and the rest of the family followed his example for the silent prayer before the meal. When he lifted his head, the conversation began. Bowls were passed, spoons scooped food onto the plates, and the events of the day began to unfold as the conversation flowed.

"Saw some of the neighbor women with their daughters in town today," Daed said, glancing at Priscilla. "They were looking through fabric at the stores."

Mamm met his gaze. "Starting to prepare for winter quilting, I reckon." Her eyes flickered over to Priscilla. "I really do think that we should be considering making a quilt this winter, Priscilla."

She caught her breath. If making applesauce was her favorite autumn activity, quilting was her favorite winter one. But she hadn't thought that the quilting bee she might attend this winter would be her own. For a moment, she didn't know how to respond. While she had only been to three quilting bees, she remembered how special those days had been. With grey winter skies appearing so dreary, it was wonderful to be surrounded by colorful fabrics, beautiful stitching, and lively women. "A quilt?" she asked. "For me?"

Daed frowned as if deep in thought as he teased her by saying, "I suppose that hope chest of yours is a bit empty!"

"Daed!" Priscilla said, glancing around the room at the rest of her family. They were laughing at her discomfort. "It'll be filled in due time, I reckon," she added softly.

"Aw, you can worry about filling it later," Jonas said, trying to change the subject. He was always the great protector of his younger sister. "Here's something a bit more current. There's a volley ball game tomorrow at the Millers," Jonas said, looking over the table at Priscilla. "I suspect you are already going, ja?"

The look on Priscilla's face made it clear that she knew nothing about the event. "I...I hadn't heard about it." She wondered whether or not Stephen was going. He hadn't mentioned it to her. Usually he would ask her if he could pick her up beforehand but, apparently, not this time. In fact, she realized, she hadn't seen him all week.

Jonas' cheeks turned pink and he looked back at his plate. "Well, I'm going to head over there after chores. I'd be happy to take you, if you want."

Mamm smiled understandingly at Priscilla. "Nothing wrong with riding along in your brother's buggy, now," she said. But the unspoken feeling was that everyone knew Priscilla was thinking about Stephen. Why hadn't he asked her?

"Ja, I reckon," Priscilla said soft, poking at her food with her fork.

"Better than Daed taking you," Jonas said with a smirk.

"Don't be cheeky," Mamm reprimanded her son but her eyes twinkled at Jonas' attempt to break the tension that had suddenly befallen the table.

"What's wrong with her daed taking her?" Daed chimed in, a pretend look of hurt on his face.

"Oh Daed," Priscilla said, smiling appreciatively at her family. She was glad that they hadn't mentioned Stephen's name but even more glad that they cared enough to remind her of what was really important in their family: each other.

Chapter Two

It was just after nine in the morning when Jonas harnessed the horse up to the special hauling buggy. It had the regular box-like front to it but the back was open and flat which would allow them to haul the apples from market back to the farm.

After Priscilla had finished her morning chores, she hurried over to Elsie's to collect Katie, Ben, and Ruth Ann for her Mamm to watch. The children held hands as they crossed the street before racing down the driveway toward the main farmhouse. A day with their *grossmammi* meant a day filled with cookies, laughter and other special treats. Priscilla smiled, watching Ruth Ann try to keep up with her older siblings. But her small little legs couldn't just quite do it.

Scooping the little girl into her arms, Priscilla nuzzled at her niece's neck. "Come, Ruth Ann," she said. "I'll get you there in no time. Can't have you missing mid-morning cookies now, can I?"

Inside the house, Katie and Ben were already seated at the old farmer's table, waiting impatiently for Mamm to place a plate of sugar cookies before them. "Hurry, Ruth Ann!" Katie snapped. "We can't get cookies until you sit down!"

Priscilla laughed. It was clear that Mamm was one step ahead of her grandchildren and was making them wait for Ruth Ann before anyone received any cookies. She set the little girl on the floor and watched as she scrambled onto the bench beside Ben. "Ready!" she exclaimed happily.

"I think Jonas is ready, Mamm," Priscilla said.

"Where you going?" Ben asked, cookie crumbs spraying across the table.

"To get apples and don't talk with your mouth full," Priscilla said.

"I want to go!" Ben cried out.

"Me, too! Me, too!" Ruth Ann piped in.

"Now, now," Mamm said, placing a small cup of cold milk by each child's plate. "If you all go, we won't have room for the apples. What's more important? That you ride along or that we have enough apples to make applesauce?"

Neither child answered but Ben scowled, knowing that his *grossmammi* was right.

The market was only twenty minutes away from the farm. Priscilla leaned her head against the door and shut her eyes. She had awoken at five in the morning to get a head start on her chores and prepare all of the items that she would need to make applesauce. It was a nice cool day for which she was thankful. But she was tired so she let the buggy gently rock her into a short nap along the way.

Truth be told, she hadn't slept much the previous night. She had tossed and turned in bed, wondering if Stephen Esh was going to show up at the volleyball game. If he did, that certainly was a sign that he wasn't as keen on courting her as she had thought. While there wasn't anything she could do about it, her heart felt heavy at the prospect.

"Wake up, sleepy head," Jonas whispered as he nudged her. "We're here."

Blinking her eyes, Priscilla lifted her head and looked around. She had forgotten where she was and it took her a moment to reorient herself. The market. Apples. With a sigh, she pushed away any thought of Stephen Esh and hurried out of the buggy to follow Jonas into the market.

It was crowded at this time of the day. Many of the women were there to gather their fruits and vegetables so that they, too, could can them for the upcoming winter months. Priscilla smiled at a few of the women from their own church district but hurried toward the back of the store where she knew that the baskets of apples were waiting. She knew that they needed ten bushels in order to make a year's worth of applesauce. It was a good thing that Jonas had brought the hauling buggy, she thought.

"Priscilla Smucker!"

At the sound of her name, Priscilla turned around. Her friend Sarah greeted her with a warm smile. "*Gude Mariye*, Sarah," Priscilla said. "You here for apples, too?"

Sarah laughed. "Ten bushels?"

Priscilla joined her. "Ten bushels!"

"Seems like we both have a long day ahead of us, ja?" Sarah glanced over her shoulder, noticing that they were alone in the aisle at the store. "You going to the volley ball game tonight?"

At the mention of the game, Priscilla sobered. She felt as if a dark cloud was passing over her head. "Brother Jonas will be taking me, ja," was her simple response.

"Jonas?" Sarah asked, lifting an eyebrow. The meaning behind Priscilla's words registered with Sarah and she sighed. Clearly Stephen was not taking Priscilla. "Well, that's what big brothers are for, anyway. We'll have a good time so it doesn't matter."

Priscilla tried to smile. "Have fun making all of your

applesauce with your mamm," she said before she turned back to the task at hand. But her heart was heavy and her pulse quickened. She felt helpless about the situation but she'd never be so brazen as to approach Stephen Esh. He was a grown man and had the right to choose whether or not he wished to court her.

It took her and Jonas five trips to carry the bushels to the hauling buggy. With everything secured, Jonas helped Priscilla into the buggy before he climbed in next to her and took the reins. With a click of his tongue and a slap of the reins on the horse's croup, Jonas steered the horse and buggy out of the parking lot and back onto the lane.

"Sure is a lot of apples, back there" he said lightly. "Can't say I'd be excited about peeling all of them."

"Good thing Katie and Ben are there today. Mayhaps they can help, ja?" she said. "After all, many hands make light the work!"

Another buggy was approaching them. As they started to pass, Jonas slowed his horse down and raised his hand to wave at the other driver. As his hand was against the window, the two buggies were closer and Jonas caught his breath. He glanced nervously at Priscilla who was staring out of the side window. At the noise of her brother gasping, she turned around just in time to catch sight of the buggy passing alongside theirs.

"Jonas!" she whispered, clutching at his arm. "Please tell me that wasn't..."

Jonas stared straight ahead, the color drained from his face. With a somber face, he clenched his jaw and said nothing.

"Jonas? Was that Susie Byler riding in Stephen Esh's

buggy toward market?" Her voice was pleading and tears began to well up in the corner of her eyes. With all of her strength, she willed Jonas to tell her that she was imagining things. But, when Jonas failed to reply again, she knew that his silence was a confirmation that, indeed, they had witnessed Stephen with another girl.

But it wasn't just any other girl. It was Susie Byler. Earlier in the summer, she had created such a horrible mess over Priscilla's donation to the Mennonite charity dinner. She had donated a decorated basket filled with tomatoes from her garden. But Susie had been jealous. The year before, Susie had earned recognition for her own donations. She hadn't liked the competition from Priscilla. Indeed, she had accused Priscilla of stealing her gardening secrets and even vandalizing her tomato garden. Susie had even demanded from Polly, the organizer of the Amish participants in the event, not to allow Priscilla to participate in the charity dinner at all. But Polly had stood firm. Unfortunately, the youth group had splintered, with several of the young women siding with Susie Byler.

It had been a horrible few months for Priscilla. The fact that anyone in the community would believe that she could have done such terrible things was extremely hurtful, to say the least. But Priscilla was not one to come right out and accuse Susie Byler of lying. She firmly believed in turning the other cheek, as did her family and the members of her community.

The only saving grace had been Stephen Esh. That had been around the time when they had started courting. She had suspected that Susie might have also been jealous of his attention being directed at Priscilla. Without Stephen's emotional support, Priscilla didn't know how she would have survived the bullying from Susie Byler. For weeks it had continued until the actual charity dinner ended and the bishop had addressed the issue of competition among the people with the congregation.

Now, to see Stephen Esh taking Susie Byler to market was especially hurtful. It was all she could do to wonder if Susie was behind Stephen not asking her to the volleyball game. If she arrived at the game and he was there with Susie, Priscilla knew that her heart would just flip-flop inside of her chest. But she also knew that Stephen had the choice and she was not one to stop him from selecting which young woman would ride in his buggy. She only wished it wasn't Susie Byler.

Back at the farm, Priscilla did her very best to push any thought of Stephen out of her mind. What's done is done, she told herself, despite the fact that her chest felt tight and the happiness was definitely gone from her day. She avoided her brother's concerned gaze as she slid open the buggy door and hurried into the sunshine, hoping its rays would help hide the tears that threatened to fall down her cheeks momentarily.

The children ran out the door and into the porch to greet her, young Ben jumping up and down and clamoring for a fresh apple to eat. Even Ruth Ann was smiling and clapping her small hands, asking for a Granny Smith to sink her teeth into, a big smile on her cherubic face.

"Apples! Apples!" Ruth Ann chanted in her baby voice with a slight lisp.

"Now, now," Jonas scolded gently. "Let me carry the baskets inside first. And they need to be washed before you eat them, ja?"

Ben made a face. "Don't like waiting."

Despite having a heavy heart, Priscilla tried to focus on

making applesauce. "We have a lot of work to do," she said with false cheerfulness in her voice. "I'm sure you'll be sick of apples by the end of the day!"

For the next hour, they set to work cleaning and preparing the apples. Priscilla showed Katie how to peel the apples and taught Ben how to core and cut them into neat, even slices, close to the core, so that the least amount of apple was wasted. The peelings were gathered together and dumped into a big bucket. They'd feed those to the chickens later.

By the end of the day, 155 jars of applesauce were lined up on the shelves, ready for use over the next year. Some would be given as gifts to the elderly for their birthdays. Others would be taken to family gatherings. One thing was certain, there would be no applesauce left over and, in twelve months, it would be time to start canning applesauce all over again.

"Just wait until Mamm hears about this," Ben said, his small hands tugging at the suspenders that held up his black pants. "She won't believe all the work we done!"

"Did," Priscilla corrected gently. "The work we did."

"Aw," he scoffed, waving his hand at his aunt. "She knows what I mean, anyway!"

"Don't be sassy, Ben!" Katie scolded.

"Don't be bossy!" Ben shot back.

The friendly, cooperative energy of the day quickly began to dissipate. Priscilla didn't want the two children to argue and ruin what had been a wonderfully welcomed distraction for her. So, she tried to divert their attention. "What an achievement we made, ja? I could never have done it without your help. What do you say that we pack up some of these jars for your mamm? I bet you'd like to taste some of this applesauce at your own home, later on tonight."

Both children lit up, their eyes sparkling and smiles on their lips. Priscilla told them to select four jars each to set on the counter while she hurried to the pantry in search of a sturdy box to carry the jars to Elsie's home when she'd walk the children across the lane.

Jonas opened the side door and poked his head inside, smiling at the children. "You little ones ready to go home?"

"Ja!" Ben shouted as he ran toward the door. He scurried under his uncle's arm and leapt off of the porch. He landed in the grass on his knees.

"Careful, now," Jonas said, laughing at the antics of the small boy.

Priscilla lifted the box from the counter. "I thought I'd walk them home."

He waved his hand at her and reached for the box. "I suspect Mamm might need some help with making supper and you might need time to get ready for the volleyball game, ja?"

What a good brother Jonas is, Priscilla thought to herself. He knew that she was still feeling poorly about seeing Susie Byler riding in Stephen's buggy. The disappointment and hurt had been easy to hide during the day with the children helping her make applesauce but clearly she needed a few minutes by herself in order to prepare for the evening. She dreaded seeing Stephen arrive with Susie in his buggy. Even worse, Priscilla felt her stomach twist at the thought of Susie Byler's smugness if she showed up with Stephen by her side.

"*Danke, brudder,*" she whispered with a shy smile. "That's right gut of you."

She watched as Jonas shifted the box so that it rested on

his hip while he reached for Ruth Ann's hand. "Let's go see your mamm," he said cheerfully. Standing in the doorway, Priscilla stared after them, her brother Jonas leading the way down the road with the three *kinner* in tow.

Indeed, she was thankful for the few extra minutes to collect her thoughts as she prepared for the evening's festivities. With so much on her mind, she needed that time to make certain that she could face the fact that she had, indeed, seen Susie Byler riding in Stephen Esh's buggy that same morning. The thought did break her heart but she refused to let it break her spirit. Life will go on, she told herself, despite the fact that she had a real hard time actually believing it.

Chapter Three

Priscilla took a deep breath before she climbed down from the buggy. Jonas gave her a reassuring smile before he hurried to hitch the horse alongside the Miller's barn where other horses were already standing. Part of her wanted to wait for Jonas but a little voice inside of her whispered, "*Face this alone.*"

She listened to the little voice.

The volleyball net was set up alongside the farmhouse. There was a long table laden with pies and pretzels as well as pitchers of lemonade and water. Several people were already playing volleyball, mostly the young men, while the women stood along the sidelines in small groups. Occasionally, several of the young women would join the game but, for the most part, it was dominated by the men.

Looking around the room, she was relieved to see her friend, Anna Zook, standing with Polly and Sarah on the other side of the volleyball net. She hurried over to join them, her eyes looking straight ahead for fear of seeing Susie Byler or Stephen Esh. Her heart was racing, hoping against all hope that neither one of them would show up.

Don't be so silly, she scolded herself. *If Susie is what Stephen wants in a girlfriend, you should be happy for him.* Yet, Priscilla knew that this wasn't the problem. She'd be happy for Stephen, no matter who he courted. He had been nothing but kind to her. She had no hard feelings toward him. However, the truth was that she knew she would never be happy for Susie Byler if she were to become the woman chosen by Stephen.

"There you are!" Anna said and reached out joyfully to hold Priscilla's hand.

"How did your applesauce making go?" Sarah asked.

"Sweet," Priscilla said lightly, despite not feeling in a teasing mood. She knew better than to let others see how torn up she was really feeling inside. Besides, she figured, she couldn't change anything and feeling gloomy would not help the situation.

"Glad to hear it," Sarah said and smiled sympathetically.

Priscilla wondered if Sarah had seen Susie with Stephen at the market. The thought made her heart quicken again and she looked away, doing her best to blink back the tears that threatened to blur her vision.

Anna didn't notice the undercurrent of the conversation. Instead, she leaned forward. "Heard that some of the women folk are starting quilting bees in the next few weeks for the fall weddings!" She looked over at Priscilla. "Mayhaps you'll be one of them, ja?"

This time, the color drained from Priscilla's face. How could she tell them about Stephen in the buggy with Susie? "I'm not quite seventeen, Anna," she said slowly, trying to act natural. "Not thinking about quilts or weddings just yet."

Sarah jumped to Priscilla's defense. "Such nonsense," she said waving her hand. "Those women just look for an excuse to quilt. Helps the winter months pass by quicker, ain't so?" She smiled at Priscilla. "Has truly nothing to do with weddings or whatnot."

Anna laughed. "I sure know my mamm isn't thinking about a quilt for me, that's for sure and certain." She leaned forward. "But I heard talk that she asked to borrow my mamm's quilting frame."

The talk was too much for Priscilla. She swallowed and looked around at her friends. Polly and Sarah were older and, by all rights, should be the ones talking about wedding quilts and quilting bees. But, truth be told, Priscilla had been looking forward to the possibility. After all, wasn't it only the evening before when her mamm had suggested that they think about it?

"I think I'll go get some lemonade," she mumbled and hurried away, hoping that a moment of peace would help her catch her breath and regain her composure.

At the food table, she poured herself a cup of lemonade and carried it over to an empty picnic table under a large oak tree. The leaves were just beginning to lose their bright green color and several had a hint of yellow starting to poke through. For a moment, she shut her eyes and enjoyed the cool air from the evening as it caressed her face. It helped to calm her down from the earlier moments of anxiety.

"I was hoping you'd be here," a voice said softly into her ear.

Priscilla opened her eyes and looked up. It was Stephen Esh, smiling at her, his hands in his pockets and his eyes sparkling. "Oh," she gasped, surprised by more than his sudden appearance. She couldn't imagine why he was talking to her if he was, indeed, interested in Susie Byler.

"I haven't seen you all week," he said. "I was hoping you'd let me take you home, Priscilla," he said softly so that no one else could hear. "After the volleyball game, I mean."

"I...but..." she stammered.

"But what?" he asked, a confused look crossing his face. "You didn't promise someone else, did you?" He looked concerned.

Now it was Priscilla's turn to frown. How could he think of such a thing? "Of course not but..." She glanced over her shoulder, wishing that someone would come rescue her. But everyone was engrossed in their own conversations. When she looked back at Stephen, he was staring at her, waiting for her to continue her sentence. "What about Susie?" she said, her voice lowered.

He frowned, his eyebrows furrowed together. His reaction made it clear that he didn't know what she meant. "Susie?"

Priscilla felt foolish and lowered her eyes. She could barely look at him. Certainly he must think that this was very forward of her. But he had asked. "Susie Byler. You took her to market this morning, ain't so?"

For a moment, Stephen was silent. It was pure curiosity that caused Priscilla to peek up at him. She expected him to be angry with her, disappointed in her question about something that was clearly none of her business. When her eyes met his, she was both surprised and relieved to see him smiling at her.

He knelt down beside the picnic table and, with a quick glance to make certain no one was watching, he reached for her hand. His thumb caressed her skin and she felt goose bumps travel up her arm. No one had ever held her hand before. His skin felt warm and the pressure of his thumb felt strong yet gentle.

"You listen to me, Priscilla Smucker," he said softly. "I know you're young, mayhaps too young to think about the future, but I want you to know that it's my hope to share in that future. With you. Not now, but some day." He glanced around again before leaning forward and kissing the top of her hand. It was a quick movement, one that caused her to catch her breath. When he looked back at her, he smiled. "You have nothing to fear about Susie Byler. I don't want to talk poorly about anyone in our community but, just know, you're a class act, Priscilla Smucker, and you've stolen my heart."

"Oh," she gasped quietly, the color flooding to her cheeks. *You've stolen my heart.* The words echoed in her ears. Did he really just say that to her?

Then, without further comment, he released her hand and stood up. She could hear the joints in his knees crack. He glanced back over at the group of young men. "Best get back to my friends, ja?" he said as he looked down at her. "I'll be saving you that seat in my buggy, Priscilla. Tonight and every night. No need for you to worry about that."

She watched as he walked away from her, rejoining his friends. Just before standing beside them, he turned around, his eyes drifting over to her one more time and he winked before turning back to the young men who stood beside him.

It took her a moment to understand what had just happened. His words had been so sweet and reassuring. No one had ever spoken to her like that before. Yet, she was confused. Hadn't she seen Stephen driving a buggy with Susie Byler sitting next to him? Clearly, Stephen was telling her that she had no competition with Susie, not for his affections anyway. And his words insinuated that he was, indeed, looking forward to the future, waiting for her to be old enough to marry.

Marry, she thought. A warm feeling spread throughout her veins. Was Stephen Esh really thinking about marrying her? She bit her lip and tried to hide her joy. No girl could do better than to have the affection and attention of Stephen Esh. She was honored and said a quick, silent prayer, asking that she'd always remain worthy of his heart.

Anna was hurrying across the grass toward her. Her face was drawn and pale. The serious expression and her determination caused Priscilla to drift away from her dreams of the future and return to the present.

"Anna? What's wrong?"

Anna took Priscilla's arm and helped her to her feet. "I need to talk to you, right now" she whispered.

Quickly, Anna led her behind the barn. There was an urgency to Anna's steps that Priscilla didn't understand. Once they were out of earshot, Anna turned to Priscilla.

"It's that Susie Byler again," she hissed. "She's at it again."

Priscilla sighed. Just what she *didn't* want to hear. "What is it this time?"

Anna took a deep breath. "*Ach vell,* she's still going on and on about the charity dinner and telling people what you did."

"I didn't do anything," Priscilla said, frustration in her voice.

"You and I know that but she keeps going on about it," Anna said, shaking her head. "But this time, she's boasting that Stephen Esh came calling on her!"

The color drained from Priscilla's face. Courting was a private matter, shared between two people with a great affinity for each other. This was done somewhat discreetly so that there would be no shame if the courtship did not last. To

30

publically speak of "courting" was immoral and prideful. It also could create a lot of problems for Stephen, especially if the people thought he was courting two girls at once. His reputation would be gravely affected. Even worse, the bishop might get involved. It wasn't a common occurrence but Priscilla knew that it had happened before in their community.

"Why would she do that?" It wasn't just that Susie was hurting Priscilla this time. Now, she was targeting Stephen, too.

Anna shook her head. "I just don't know, Priscilla. But she was telling Rachel and Linda that he's courting her, not you."

This time, she gasped. Why would Susie Byler stoop so low as to mention Priscilla's name when spreading her horrid gossip and prideful claims? "Oh! She makes me so angry," Priscilla whispered. "I don't feel Christian when I hear her name."

"Me neither," Anna confessed. "She's just not a nice person at all."

With a big sigh, Priscilla reached out and took Anna's hand in hers. She met her friend's eyes and tried to smile. "We just have to try harder, I reckon. Jesus taught us to love the sinners, didn't he?"

Anna squeezed her friend's hand. "You are right, Priscilla. We have to try harder." But she couldn't help adding, "Despite Susie making it really difficult to do just that."

They both laughed and gave each other a quick, friendly hug. Priscilla was glad to have such a good friend as Anna. It made the hard times much easier to survive when there was a person like Anna in her life.

"Now, let's go join that volleyball game and show those

other girls what fun is all about," Anna said confidently. "And standing on the sidelines sure isn't it!"

Together, they walked over to where the game was being played and joined a side. For the next hour, they laughed with the other youth and enjoyed themselves, quickly forgetting about Susie Byler and her antics.

Chapter Four

Stephen helped Priscilla into the buggy after the volleyball game. He made certain that she was situated and comfortable before he closed the door and latched it. Then he hurried around to the other side. She noticed that he paused to rub his hand down his horse's neck, a simple gesture that spoke volumes about his character.

Once he was beside her and had the horse moving, she felt herself relax. She berated herself for having doubted Stephen's intentions although she was still curious about Susie's presence in his buggy earlier that day. And why, she wondered, would Susie be boasting that Stephen had 'come calling' at her home. However, she knew that such questions were not to be asked. Either she trusted Stephen or she didn't. She certainly wasn't about to ask the questions that were running through her mind. That would be stooping to the level of Susie Byler. Unlike Susie, Priscilla was not about to start rumors or spread lies.

"I've been busy this past week," he said, finally breaking the silence in the buggy. The horse trotted down the road, the sound of its hooves clipping against the macadam in a gentle rhythm. Stephen glanced at Priscilla as he added, "Daed really needed my help since brother Eli has been visiting relatives in Ohio."

Ah, she thought. So that explains why she hadn't seen much of him.

"And one of the neighbor's has been feeling poorly so I offered to help with the morning and evening milking," he continued.

"Oh Stephen," she exclaimed. Now that she understood why he hadn't been over to see her, she was worried about how hard he was working. Helping his daed and a neighbor meant long days and short nights. "That's so much work for you!"

He shrugged lightly. "Idle hands are no gut."

That was Stephen. A good, solid Amish man. Rather than admit that he was working too hard, he turned it around to seem as if it were the most natural thing in the world to work sixteen to eighteen hour days because his help was needed by his daed and his daed's neighbor. He always put others' needs before his own. If ever a man upheld the Lord's Commandments, it ought to be Stephen Esh. She made a silent promise to herself to continue trying to be more like him so that she would be worthy of making him proud of her.

"And your own farm?"

He looked at her and smiled. "All's gut," he said. "Just glad it's autumn already. No crops to harvest." A car slowed down behind the buggy and passed them. Stephen moved the horse over to the side of the road, giving a wide berth to the fast moving automobile. "Next spring will be different," he admitted. "I want to double the crops so that there is a big corn harvest in the summer. I may have to hire some help."

"Is that economical?" she heard herself ask, immediately wishing she could retract the question. She didn't want him to think that she was nosy about his business.

But Stephen merely took a deep breath and lifted his shoulders. "I keep asking myself the same question, Priscilla. But I can't let down my daed. Even if I make less money per acre, it will still be more than what I can do on my own, ain't that so?"

There was sense in what he explained. Priscilla found herself impressed by his business sense. "You do have a point, Stephen. Can't argue that."

There was a moment of silence. She listened to the sounds of the horse and buggy, relaxing as she sat next to Stephen. She couldn't imagine the workload that he had taken on during the past few weeks. Working for his daed, managing his own farm, and helping a neighbor. No one could ever accuse Stephen Esh of having idle hands, that was for sure and certain.

Her thoughts were interrupted when he cleared his throat and said, "I heard the women were making applesauce this week. Did you?"

Priscilla nodded, happy to move into safer territory and something she was comfortable discussing. "Oh ja!" she gushed. "Jonas and I picked up ten bushels this morning and I spent all day with Mamm and two of sister Elsie's *kinner* peeling, cooking, and canning the apples. Little Katie and Ben were such a big help. I think Ben felt most important that he had the chopping job."

A broad grin crossed Stephen's face. "Aw, Priscilla," he said. "That's mighty gut of you! Letting the little ones help out and making them feel gut about themselves. He'll remember that long after the applesauce is all eaten, ja?"

There was a long pause and Priscilla could tell that Stephen was thinking hard about something. His brow was furrowed and he chewed on his bottom lip. "Speaking of applesauce, you mentioned that you saw me when I took Susie Byler to market today to buy apples. Her daed's been ill and

I've been helping out at their farm." He glanced at Priscilla. "She doesn't have any brothers, you know."

Without realizing it, Priscilla exhaled. She felt as if a big weight had been lifted from her shoulders. "That's the neighbor you were mentioning earlier?"

Stephen nodded. "Ja, her daed is right sick with a bad flu. Could hardly get out of bed this week. I offered to help with the milking. Seemed like the neighborly thing to do."

"Of course," Priscilla said and nodded emphatically, fighting the shadow of shame that threatened to wash over her for having been jealous and doubting Stephen.

"I was there last evening milking the cows. Just as I was leaving, Susie asked if I could take her to the market for the apples. I felt I couldn't say no," he explained, his eyes meeting Priscilla's. "That's why I haven't been over to you, Priscilla. I've been busy helping the Bylers." He paused before he lowered his voice and added, "And I certainly haven't been calling on Susie or anyone else but you."

So he had heard about Susie's mean-spirited boasting! He must have suspected that those boasts had reached Priscilla's ears and wanted to stop any gossip before it grew larger and took on a life of its own.

Tears came to Priscilla's eyes, despite her fierce determination to fight them. She was glad that it was dark and he couldn't see. She didn't want to let him know that she had doubted his intentions. "I see," she whispered.

He stopped the buggy and looked over at her. It was dark in the buggy but the light from the headlights cast a soft glow so that she could see him staring at her. He had a serious look on his face as he continued. "I meant what I said earlier,

36

Priscilla. And..." He paused again. She waited patiently for him to continue, sensing that what he had to say was very important. "I also know that everyone is talking about winter quilting."

She caught her breath but didn't say anything.

"Well, I know it's soon but..." He cleared his throat. He seemed nervous. That was a first, she thought. Stephen was always so sure of himself. "It might not be a bad idea if you...well, you could certainly start your quilt...if you'd like."

"Oh..." she said, her throat constricting and the word coming out in a breathless whoosh.

"I mean...well...only if you wanted to," he stammered nervously. "Or not, I guess."

"It is rather soon," she said quietly. She could sense that he tensed beside her. "But I...I think that might be a nice idea," she quickly added. "A quilting bee, I mean."

She felt his relief. He reached over and touched her hand. "And what about the future, Priscilla? With a finished quilt, perhaps we could put it to good use next December then?"

"December?" Her heart was racing. That was over a year away. But it wasn't uncommon for the younger women to know that far in advance of the intention of a young man. "If that's what you'd like," she whispered. "I wouldn't be eighteen yet."

He laughed and lifted her hand to his lips again. Pressing a soft kiss against her skin, he said, "I don't want you to worry about anyone or anything, Priscilla Smucker. I want you to be Stephen's Priscilla and I don't care who knows, even if it is a long way away." He released her hand. "It will give me time to prepare the farm and for us to court more openly, ja?"

She wanted to laugh, to tell him how relieved she was. But the words wouldn't form on her lips. Instead, she nodded her head, despite the fact that he couldn't see her. "I won't worry anymore, Stephen," she said softly. "And I'd like nothing more than to be Stephen's Priscilla."

And, with that, she knew the path of her future. With joy, they rode the rest of the way to the Smucker farm in silence, both thinking about the commitment they had just made to each other and reveling in the knowledge that forever was just beginning for the two of them.

Chapter Five

"So I was thinking," Priscilla said casually to her Mamm. It was Wednesday, four days after her talk with Stephen about his intentions. They were in the kitchen making cheese. Her mamm was busy slicing the curds into large chunks that would be pressed into big, round wheels later in the afternoon. Priscilla was leaning against the sink, idly drying the dishes from the noon meal. "Mayhaps making that quilt this winter would be a right gut idea."

Out of the corner of her eye, Priscilla saw her mamm stop for a moment. Her back stiffened and she was silent. Then, as if she hadn't paused, she began sliding the long knife back through the curds. "I see," she said, glancing over her shoulder at Priscilla. "You know, nowadays many of the young women are opting to put store bought comforters inside their hope chests instead of home-made quilts."

Even though her mother couldn't see, Priscilla shrugged her shoulders. She had heard about this trend and didn't think much of it. "Well, I think I much prefer a quilt. Means much more to have so many women helping to make it, ja?"

Her mamm set the knife on the side of the stove and turned around. "Priscilla," she said softly. Her eyes were soft and full of love. "I couldn't agree with you more. I'd be more than happy to have a quilting bee for your wedding quilt."

Priscilla bit her lip. *Wedding quilt.* The words echoed in her head. It sounded strange. "Well, mayhaps we could just call it a quilt for my hope chest," she offered. "I'd feel awfully brazen calling it a wedding quilt."

"Brazen?" her mamm asked. There was a hint of a smile on her mamm's face but she didn't inquire further than a raised eyebrow.

"*Ja vell*," Priscilla responded. A wedding quilt usually meant that the couple had announced their intentions at church or, at least, had both been baptized already, with their eyes looking toward the future. Since Priscilla wouldn't be taking her baptism until the spring or even autumn of the following year, marriage was definitely not in the near future. He had said December of next year. Plenty of time to get to know each other better without the worry of Susie Byler trying to create waves or drive a wedge between them. "It would be a long while before a wedding, anyway."

"I see," her mamm said again, nodding her head in approval. As if reading her daughter's mind, Mamm added, "Especially since you haven't taken your baptism yet, I reckon you're right."

It was on Saturday when Priscilla had time to sit down with her Mamm to discuss the quilting bee again. They had to decide about the pattern and the colors before heading to the local fabric store. It would be a hard few weeks as Mamm and Priscilla would have to cut and piece the quilt top. That needed to be completed before they could start the actual quilting. It wouldn't be until November when the quilting frame would be set up and the women invited on Saturday afternoons for fellowship and time spent together stitching the pattern of the quilt. With the holidays, the quilt wouldn't be finished until January or February, the perfect time to finish as the spring preparation chores would begin at that time.

"I was thinking of your mamm's pattern," Priscilla said shyly. "The same one that you had and the one that she had.

40

What is it called? Eureka? It would mean ever so much to me to have the same pattern on my own bed one day."

Mamm blinked. "That pattern is rather complicated, Priscilla. The more dense the quilting, the longer it will take to quilt it. And the top will take a long time to piece."

"Just means more time together, ain't so?"

Mamm smiled and reached out to pat her daughter's hand. "You are such a gut daughter, Priscilla," she said. "And you'll certainly make a gut wife."

Priscilla blushed. She still hadn't wrapped her arms around the fact that Stephen Esh had made his intentions known to her. *Stephen's Priscilla*, she thought, a warm feeling flowing throughout her body. She quickly changed her thoughts and got back to the quilt. "I was thinking of a white and green quilt...maybe with the accent pieces in blue or a burgundy. What do you think, Mamm?"

Her mother nodded. "Those are good colors, Priscilla. Not too feminine and a good representation of the earthly blessings we are given by the Lord."

For the rest of the day, they planned out the different fabrics they would need and sketched out a design. After the noon meal, Priscilla helped Jonas hitch up the buggy to the horse so that she and Mamm could ride to the fabric stores to start searching for cloth. It would take weeks to piece the quilt top but Priscilla was looking forward to it. She loved working with fabric and sewing the pieces together would pass the time during the upcoming cold and grey afternoons.

"I reckon it will be a few weeks before we can begin quilting," Mamm said as they walked through the fabric store. "But I'll let the women know on Church Sunday. Want to make certain they plan on coming to the farm."

Priscilla ran her hand over a dark green floral bolt of cloth. "What about this mamm?"

"Priscilla Smucker!" someone called out.

She looked up, startled to see one of her friends approach. "Naomi! How are you?"

"Why I'm just fine," she said. She glanced at the fabric in Priscilla's hands. "That's not for a new dress now, is it?"

Mamm smiled. "We're making a wedding quilt this winter for Priscilla," she said.

Naomi frowned as she digested the words. Priscilla gave an inward groan. Naomi was one of the young women who straddled the fence when it came to the subject of Susie Byler. Certainly that morsel of information from her mamm would be repeated in no time to Susie. Priscilla could only imagine what Susie's reaction would be, especially since she had been so open about her claims on Stephen at the volleyball game last weekend.

"A wedding quilt?"

"Lots of young women are making them," Priscilla was quick to add.

"I see," Naomi said, her grey eyes flashing. "Well, that's sure a lovely fabric you have picked out, Priscilla."

"*Danke*," Priscilla said. "We'll see you at church tomorrow, ja?"

Mamm added, "And make certain to come to the quilting bee. Won't be for a few weeks but we'll hold them on Saturdays on the weekends we don't have service."

"I wouldn't miss it," Naomi said and smiled before she

turned around and hurried back to her own shopping.

Mamm glanced down at the fabric in Priscilla's hand. "That's is a nice piece of cloth, isn't it?" she said.

But Priscilla wasn't thinking about the cloth anymore. She was envisioning how Susie would react. Naomi was sure to tell her about the "wedding" quilt. She could only imagine how embarrassed Susie would feel after having told people that Stephen had come calling on her. With a pit in her stomach, Priscilla tried to push away the doom and gloom image of Susie's reaction. But it lingered there, too close to the surface to be dismissed.

Chapter Six

It was late November and the sky was gloomy and dark. The clouds creating a solid cover that hindered the sun from poking through in order to warm the ground. It looked cold outside and Priscilla was happy that she was going to be inside for the most part of the day.

The women had started arriving shortly after ten in the morning. For the past two days, Priscilla had been helping her mamm prepare for the first day of their quilting bee. They had enlisted the help of David and Jonas to move the larger furniture out of the gathering room next to the kitchen. After everything was empty, Priscilla had cleaned the downstairs, making certain that everything was spic and span, no dust hidden in any corners or windowsills.

Mamm had inspected every thing with an eagle's eye. "Won't do to have anyone think that I can't keep my house properly," she mumbled to Priscilla as she examined even the smallest nook and cranny. Finally, she nodded her approval. "That'll do, Priscilla."

Despite the lack of praise, Priscilla knew that her mamm was pleased with her hard work.

Next, the men had put together the quilting frame. It took up the larger part of the room. Around it, Priscilla set up chairs and benches. This is where the women would sit to quilt and share stories both before and after the noon meal.

For the next few months, the women would come visiting to contribute to the quilt every other Saturday. They liked to quilt only on the weeks when they didn't have church service. During the week was too hard for it was the wedding season. Many of the young couples were getting married on Tuesdays and Thursdays throughout the different communities, which meant that many families were attending weddings on those days. Some of the weddings were local to the church district, which meant that everyone attended the wedding. For those, a Saturday was the perfect quilting day.

The older women usually came earlier in the day and left after the meal while the younger ones would arrive for the meal and stay later, lingering to sing hymns while quilting and to help clean up before leaving to return to their parents' farm in time for evening chores.

Mamm and Priscilla had spent two weeks piecing the quilt top. First they had to cut the pieces of fabric then sew them together. For that, they had used the sewing machine that Mamm kept in the master bedroom. It ran off of a small solar box that Daed had set up for just this purpose.

When they had finally stretched the quilt onto the frame, Priscilla had simply stared at it. The pattern was called Eureka with a large star at the center of the fabric. But each point of the star was made out of two color squares. At the center of the star was another square with a symmetrical flower in two tones of green and two tones of red. Surrounding the star and flower were diamonds. But each diamond had something unique about the pattern. One diamond had a wavy edge while another had red starbursts.

It was such an unusual pattern with very complicated piecing of the material. One of the things about the pattern that Priscilla loved was how it covered the bed. With the pillows neatly tucked under the quilt at the to of the bed, the pattern folded over upon itself and the outer diamonds lined up perfectly with the inner ones. When the bed was made, it was stunning in the symmetry, a true display of sophisticated sewing in constructing the quilt top.

Now, as the women sat around and started quilting, they were all talking about the gorgeous pattern. Priscilla had blushed and quickly diffused the praise. "It's a pattern from my mamm and her mamm," she said quietly. "Certainly no prettier than other patterns, I'm sure."

The older women nodded their head and smiled at each other. Priscilla's response had been modest enough to gain their approval. Too often, some of the younger women were eager for praise, especially given that they were in a period of their lives when they were uncertain and insecure. But Priscilla had definitely passed that test.

The women were eager to begin the quilting process. They set their thimbles and spools of white thread on top of the quilt as they sat around the frame. One of the women had a pair of small sewing scissors on a pink string tied hanging from her neck. Another woman had set three spools of thread before her as well as a set of spare needles in a plastic bag. The older women were seasoned quilters and knew the small tricks of the trade in order to be most productive.

There was something peaceful about sitting among the quilters, listening to their stories about friends and family, stories that helped bond the women. Priscilla couldn't imagine why any young woman would prefer a store bought comforter over the magic of a hand-made, love-sewn quilt.

"Look how tiny your stitches are, dear," Lizzie Miller said. Her brown eyes were sunken in her face, the wrinkles under her eyes speaking of the many years that she had helped her husband tend to the crops in the fields. "So even and small. You must have been practicing."

Priscilla smiled at the older woman. "I love quilting, ja."

Lizzie looked up and stared across the quilting frame. Her eyes caught an older woman with white hair pulled into such a tight bun that her part was nearly a whole inch wide. "Lydia, did you hear that Mary Ruth and Jacob announced their intentions last week?"

Lydia clucked her tongue and shook her head. "Let me guess...a store bought comforter?" she asked disapprovingly, causing laughter to erupt around the room. "What is wrong with these young people anyway? Whoever heard of a store-bought covering for the marriage bed?" She looked up, her dark steely eyes penetrating those who looked at her. "A wedding quilt! That's what helps start a marriage and keep it strong all along!"

Several grey heads bobbed up and down in agreement. Priscilla smiled to herself, trying not to giggle at their seriousness over the topic.

When her eyes fell on Priscilla, Lydia softened her gaze. "A wise choice, Priscilla," she said. "You are keeping worldliness out of your home."

Mamm looked up from her needle and frowned. "Now Lydia," she chastised. "This is not a wedding quilt. It's for her hope chest."

Pressing her lips together into a tight link, Lydia waved her weathered hand. "Pfff!" she hissed. "We all know that truth. Anyone can see the intention of that young man of hers."

Color rose to Priscilla's cheeks and she lowered her eyes.

"This time next year, your daughter will be living at the farm down the lane, you mark my words!" Lydia added emphatically.

Lizzie bumped Priscilla with her arm in a gesture of gentle teasing. "You mark her words!" she laughed and the rest of the women joined her.

It was almost noon when the younger women started to arrive. They greeted the different mamms and grossmammis with handshakes and soft-spoken greetings as they walked around the room. Priscilla stood up and hurried over to welcome her friends.

"Why Priscilla," Anna gushed. "That is just the most beautiful pattern!"

Polly nodded her head. "I don't think I've even seen that pattern before."

"It's a variation of the eureka. See how it looks like a large star inside the diamond? But when you really look, you can see that the quilting pattern is really boxes," she explained. "It was passed down from my *grossmammi* to my mamm."

"Makes me want to think about putting a quilt into my hope chest," Anna said, her eyes sparkling. "Mayhaps you could help me pick my pattern and colors, ja?"

Priscilla flushed. She wasn't used to so much attention. "I'd be happy to, Anna," she responded.

Naomi and Sarah joined them. "I'm probably going to buy a nice comforter for my hope chest," Naomi said.

Someone snorted from around the quilting frame and Priscilla glanced over her shoulder at Lydia who was shaking her head and frowning. Hiding her amusement, Priscilla turned back to her friends. "We all have our own tastes, ain't so?" she said pleasantly.

"Girls," Mamm called. "Mayhaps you could get the table ready. Priscilla can help you with the food."

"Yes, Mamm."

The older women continued to talk while the younger women prepared the table. Priscilla helped to direct their efforts. She tried to listen to what the women were talking about while the younger women worked. She loved listening to their stories and gentle teasing. They would share these stories while their heads were bent over, their fingers making the smallest stitches possible in the patterns, usually 7 to 8 stitches per inch. The smaller the stitches, the more the women praised each other.

"I heard Amos Hostetler's getting married again," one of the women said.

"Again?" Lizzie gasped. "That's wife number three, ain't so?"

Someone else clucked her tongue. "With all those young kinner, he needs a wife."

Mamm sighed. "Poor Amos. Must be hard to have lost two wives."

Lizzie scoffed, her wrinkled mouth pursed together. "Odds aren't in number three's favor, I'd say."

The other women laughed at her and even Priscilla smiled. This was what she loved. The quilting bee was much more about the making of a quilt. It was about fellowship and community. It was about love and friendship. And it was about peace and God.

"Shall we sing a hymn before we eat?" Mamm asked. That was the signal for the quilting to stop. Priscilla refilled the water pitcher and set it on the table while the older women began to shuffle over to the table. After dinner, most of the older women would have a cup or two of coffee before leaving. Then, for the next hour or two, the younger women would take their turn at the quilt. But the transition was always a hymn.

Priscilla listened as the women began to sing a song from the Ausbund. The words touched her and she glanced around the room. She felt the presence of God among these wonderful women, women who had known her from birth and had watched her grow up. Now, they were helping to celebrate the next transition facing Priscilla: baptism and marriage.

She realized that the thread used to make those tiny stitches held so much more together than just a quilt. It held together the community. No store bought comforter could ever replace the magic that was felt during a quilting bee. A smile in her heart, Priscilla joined the rest of the women as they sang:

It is truly a narrow way,
Who now wants to go this heavenly path,
He must surely keep himself
That he does not stumble on the path,
Through affliction, misery, anxiety, and need,
Love must not wax cold.

He must completely depend
On God, wholly trusting in Him.
The Scriptures show clearly and plainly,
Upon God shall man securely build,
He is the rock, cornerstone, and foundation,
Whoever builds a house on Him,
No wind will blow it down.[1]

---

[1] Ausbund Song 51, verse 2.

Chapter Seven

"She said what?" Priscilla gasped.

It was Saturday afternoon and Anna and Polly had come over to the farm. The sky was overcast and there was a cold breeze in the air. Since the leaves had long fallen from the trees, there was a general gloomy feeling about the day. What was worse was the fact that her friends' displayed the same level of seriousness. When Priscilla saw them standing at the door, she knew something was wrong. It was rare that both of them would just show up together without having arranged such a visit in advance. But Priscilla never could have imagined what they would tell her.

"Susie said you stole the pattern for your wedding quilt from her," Polly repeated slowly. "She's been telling everyone that and has threatened to go to the bishop."

"The bishop?" Just more bad news tossed into the mix.

Anna nodded. "I heard my daed talking about it with my uncle." Since her uncle was the bishop for their church district, Anna always knew what was going on in the community. "Don't tell him that I told you so."

"Quilting patterns are so common! How could anyone steal a pattern?" Priscilla exclaimed. "Besides, I've never even seen any of her quilts! This is absurd!"

Gently, Polly laid her hand on Priscilla's arm. "I know that. You know that." The look on her face was sympathetic but clearly puzzled. "Unfortunately, the other young women don't know that

Priscilla's hand flew to her mouth. "They're believing

her? Again?"

Anna nodded. "She's quite convincing when she's spreading falsehoods. After all, everyone knows that Stephen Esh was calling on her," she said, her voice sarcastic but driving home the point that Susie Byler had set up Priscilla to look like a thief. First she had stolen Susie's young man, now she had stolen the quilt pattern. This wasn't going to make Priscilla seem like an upstanding member of the community, that was for sure and certain.

"There's more," Polly hesitated. She glanced nervously at Anna before adding, "She claims that she's being bullied by you.

Another gasp escaped Priscilla's lips. Bullied? By me? "I cannot believe you!"

Anna nodded. "That was one of the things that my daed was talking about. The bullying."

This time, Priscilla didn't stop the tears that sprang to her eyes. "But I haven't even talked to that woman since before the charity dinner! I've been doing everything in my power to avoid her."

"That's probably feeding her anger against you," Polly said gently. "You haven't been paying any mind to her and her attention seeking ways, Priscilla. She's not as strong as you and this is her way to get your attention."

A frown crossed Priscilla's face. "My attention? Whatever for?"

Polly shrugged. "I can't say, for sure and certain, but you have such a high standing in the community and now, with Stephen Esh calling on you, she might just want to strike back at you because she's jealous and you have been so successful at avoiding her."

The entire scenario was surreal. Priscilla had never said one bad word against Susie Byler, not even after the mess she had almost made of the charity dinner. The bishop had supported Priscilla then, publically talking about the situation at a worship service and demonstrating his support by trying to outbid Stephen Esh for buying her donation to the charity auction. Certainly he would support her again, Priscilla thought.

What was even more disturbing, however, was the fact that Susie Byler seemed to have some sort of hold over other members of their youth group. They listened to her and they believed her, no matter how outlandish her claims were.

"We thought you should know," Anna said quietly.

Priscilla nodded her head, knowing that her friends were right to tell her. Certainly she would have done the same for any of her friends. But she didn't know what else to say. The fact that anyone could say such horrible things about her, especially someone she didn't know, was hurtful.

"*Danke*," she said to her two friends. "You are both gut friends to have told me." In truth, she was glad that they had found the strength to inform her. If she hadn't known about Susie's drama and lies, she'd never have been prepared to address them.

Of course, she realized, she didn't have the faintest idea of how to approach the situation. Clearly, speaking to the young woman was out of the question. Priscilla wondered if there wasn't something wrong with Susie Byler that was masking her so determined to ruin other people's reputations.

Polly took a deep breath and exhaled. "I have been

doing what I can to make certain everyone knows the truth," she said.

"Oh Polly," Priscilla said. "I'm so thankful for you but you don't have to do that." She glanced around nervously. "I don't want people talking about you as well."

With a casual wave of her hand, Polly dismissed that comment. "They can talk all they want," she said. "She can't do much to me."

Anna nodded. "She's just jealous of Stephen's attention in your direction. I think the quilting sent her over the edge."

That didn't make any sense to Priscilla. Clearly Stephen wasn't interested in Susie so why would she want to deny Stephen happiness? That was most unusual and unkind. And to try to deliberately hurt his standing in the community by making him look like he left her for Priscilla? She frowned. That couldn't be what Susie Byler was up to, she realized. In truth, she was trying to damage Priscilla's reputation so that Stephen wouldn't be able to marry her. After all, that would not be the first time, Priscilla thought. Didn't Suzie already try to destroy her reputation, even lying outright to the community and spreading unfounded rumors about her tomato patch?

A pit was growing in her stomach and she felt nauseous. Susie was willing to hurt both Stephen and Priscilla just to satisfy her own loss? How could someone harbor such hatred in her heart?

"Jealousy truly is a sin, isn't it?" Priscilla said quietly. "If it drives someone to ruin other people's lives, her jealousy must be awful powerful. I can only imagine how unhappy she must be."

"Try not to worry too much," Anna said. "Mayhaps you

should speak to the bishop tomorrow after church, ja?"

Priscilla nodded but didn't respond. She wasn't one to approach the bishop with her own problems. In fact, she hadn't done more than share with him simple pleasantries at the greeting line before the sermons on Sundays. Other than that, she hadn't had much of a need to seek his counsel or engage in conversation with him. She certainly wasn't relishing the idea of starting now, especially since she wanted to speak to him about a spring baptism. But that thought was mired in apprehension; after all, baptism was the most important commitment a young man or woman undertook in the community. One had to approach it with a clear mind and a pure heart. That commitment could not possibly be shrouded in a veil of malevolence and negative thoughts, whether or not this was the result of another member of the community or stemming from her own reaction to the deeds of the perpetrator.

Chapter Eight

The next day was Church Sunday. Priscilla felt tense and anxious. She remembered that one service during the summer when Susie Byler had been so upset about Priscilla donating her tomatoes to the Mennonite Charity Dinner. Several of the young women had been distant and cold toward her, despite the fact that Priscilla had done nothing wrong. If they had behaved that way over tomatoes, how would they behave now that Susie was accusing her of stealing a quilt pattern?

"What's ailing you, daughter?" Daed asked as she slowly picked at her food. "Feeling poorly?"

"*Nee,*" she said softly.

Jonas scoffed at her. "Bet I know what's troubling you!"

She snapped her head to glare at her brother. "Nothing is wrong, Jonas."

He made a face.

Mamm looked from one to the other. "What's going on, Priscilla? I haven't seen you so distraught since the summer."

Jonas raised an eyebrow and nodded. "I wonder if it's connected."

"Jonas!" Priscilla whispered harshly. "Don't."

Daed set his fork down and whipped his mouth with his thumb. "It's not that Jacob's daughter again," he said by way of a question.

Priscilla didn't answer.

"She's been telling everyone that Priscilla stole Stephen Esh from her and then stole her pattern for her wedding quilt from her."

"Lots of stealing going on, ja?" David chortled.

Mamm pursed her lips and glanced at her husband. "That's my mamm's pattern. Complicated but not unique." She shook her head and lowered her eyes. "Stealing quilting patterns! That's ridiculous. I never heard such nonsense!"

"Mayhaps I should have a talk with Jacob, ja?" Daed said. His eyes narrowed and he frowned. "Enough is enough with this crazy daughter of his."

Mamm gasped at Daed's words but Priscilla was quick to interject.

"*Nee*, Daed," Priscilla said, shaking her head. The last thing she wanted was for her parents to get involved. She was almost seventeen years old and needed to handle this on her own. "But *danke* anyway."

Yet, the dark shadow on his face didn't leave. "She keeps this up and she'll be an old milk maid, helping her daed at the dairy and never getting herself situated in a home of her own. And with a bad reputation, she'll be nothing more than a burden to her parents!"

"Daed!" Priscilla exclaimed, shocked once again at the vehemence with which he spoke.

He turned back toward his food, picking at it but not eating. It was clear that he was angry. "I'll not have this unchristian-like behavior against my daughter, ruining her good name!"

"Have you talked to Stephen about this?" David asked, playing with this food on his plate. "Seems he has some pull with her." He looked at his sister. "Was his attention she was after, anyhow."

She was amazed at how open everyone was being with her. Such emotions and feelings were usually kept private but the entire family had let loose regarding their feelings about Susie Byler. She was touched by their concern and desire to help her with this situation.

"I...I don't want to bother Stephen with such silliness," she said softly. He worked so hard. How could she bother him with such a trivial matter?

"May not be trivial to him," David said softly.

Her daed glowered. "After all that Stephen did for that family when Jacob was ill! Jacob would be most unhappy to learn what his daughter's been up to among the community."

As soon as they had arrived at the Hostetler farm for church service, Priscilla sensed the stares from several of the younger women. She took a deep breath and ignored their hostile looks as she greeted all of the women who stood by the worship room with a handshake and a kiss. Most of the older women smiled at her, apparently not aware of Susie's horrible lies or, if they were aware, clearly not believing any of her foolishness.

When Priscilla saw Susie standing at the end of the line among a group of young women, she immediately cut short her greetings and moved away to find her mamm. Her heart raced and she lifted her chin, hoping to convey a sense of calm that she didn't feel. She had noticed Naomi among the women that surrounded Susie Byler. Priscilla felt her pulse quicken. Hadn't Naomi been at her quilting just a few weeks ago? That would explain how Susie would know which quilt pattern Priscilla had selected since, clearly, Susie wasn't about to come for any of the quilting bees at the Smucker farm.

It was during the fellowship meal that talk returned to Priscilla's quilt. Lydia and Lizzie were talking with several of the other elderly women. Priscilla was walking along the table to make certain that everyone had their water cups filled. She was lingering near the women, reaching between Lydia and Lizzie to collect their cups.

"Now this is a sensible young woman," Lydia said, her hand reaching out to touch Priscilla's. "Have you heard about Priscilla's quilt, Katie?" she asked the woman sitting across from her. "It's the most splendid pattern and such lovely colors."

"I've heard about this quilt," Katie said. "Heard it was quite special indeed!"

Priscilla flushed. "It was my mamm's and her mamm's before that. But it's not uncommon at all," she added quickly. She glanced at the women, wondering how many of them had heard the accusations against her. But she sensed no animosity among these gentle women. Whether they had heard or not, they were not judging her or believing the slanderous lies from the jealous Susie.

Lydia spoke up. "It's gut to keep patterns in the family."

"No one owns patterns," Priscilla added softly, hoping that enough people heard.

"Well," Katie said. "I suppose I need to see this amazing quilt. I'll be certain to stop by for some quilting time next week."

Several other women nodded their heads in agreement. Priscilla realized that the talk of the quilt had traveled down the table. She noticed Susie's mother sitting among them. She kept a straight face and did not seem to contribute to the discussion. Clearly, she had her own opinions that were swayed by her daughter's perspective on the quilting situation.

Taking a deep breath, Priscilla moved away from the table and retreated to the kitchen in order to refill the water pitcher. She was sorry that she had ever decided to make this quilt. It was causing her such a headache, dealing with the public speculation and opinions. Yet, she knew when it was finished, she would have something that she would treasure forever. Unfortunately, it would be tainted by the drama that Susie Byler had created.

"Priscilla," someone said from behind.

It was the bishop. Priscilla took a deep breath and set the water pitcher down on the counter. "Bishop Zook!"

"I'd like a word in private," he said, his face expressionless and his eyes dark.

"That's gut," she said. "I was hoping to speak to you, too."

They walked outside of the kitchen in to the yard. There were several people rushing back and forth from the house to the barn where the fellowship tables had been set up. The bishop led Priscilla away from where anyone could overhear their conversation.

"I've been hearing some disturbing commentary about your behavior," he said solemnly.

Priscilla felt the color drain from her face. About *her* behavior? She wondered if she had heard him properly. "I'm sorry. I...I don't know what you are talking about."

"There has been talk of a quilt pattern, that you took the pattern from Susie Byler after her beau started courting you," the bishop said. He held up his hand to stop Priscilla from speaking, despite the fact that she was speechless. "This is not the first time your name has come to my ears. The first time, I ignored it and even supported you position as I heard that some of the accusations were false."

"But..."

He silenced her with a steely look. "For a young woman with such an upright reputation in the community, I'm surprised at you, Priscilla Smucker."

She felt the sting of tears in her eyes. "I had wanted to talk to you, Bishop, about the very same thing. Only I think you have heard a different version of the story."

"Oh?" he said, raising an eyebrow.

"That quilt pattern is my mamm's and her mamm's. I didn't steal anything, Bishop. And as far as being courted, I never heard that anyone was courting Susie Byler." Priscilla lifted her eyes to look at the bishop, fighting back the tears that threatened to roll down her cheeks. "I'm not certain of the reason for these accusations but they are false, Bishop. I fear it is to make me look poorly in the eyes of the community but I don't know why."

She wished that she could tell the bishop the truth, that Susie had spread those lies on purpose, to tell him about how Stephen had been helping Jacob Byler and Susie had decided to tell everyone that he was calling on her. However, Priscilla refused to stoop to Susie's level. She wasn't about to try to ruin anyone's reputation, even someone as mean as Susie Byler. After all, Priscilla knew that wishes of ill-doing on others often returned to the sender. The Bible was clear about that. Wasn't it in the Book of Esther when Haman was hung from the very gallows that he had constructed in order to kill Mordechai?

"I see," the bishop said, tugging at his beard. It was clear that he was perplexed by this new bit of information. "I'll have to pray on this, Priscilla."

He turned around to leave. Priscilla stared at his back as thoughts flooded through her mind. That wasn't the way that she anticipated the conversation progressing. Indeed, she had wanted to talk to him about attending the upcoming instructional for spring baptism. She had also wanted to talk to him about how to handle Susie's jealousy. But she had never intended to mention Susie's name. Instead, Priscilla had been caught off guard by the bishop's comments about her behavior.

Her eyes burned and she fought the tears that touched the corners of her eyes. Wiping at them, she looked around the room, hoping that no one had witnessed their discussion. No one seemed to have noticed the stern lecture that Priscilla had received from the bishop. Thankful for that small miracle, Priscilla tried to take a deep breath before slipping out the back door into the cold air for a moment alone in order to compose herself before she had to face the women once again.

Chapter Nine

For the next few days, Priscilla seemed to move about in a daze. She was still hurt that the bishop would have believed Susie Byler's complaint and not questioned her further or checked with her family. Having talked to him, Priscilla didn't feel any better. He was still doubtful and that bothered her. After all, for her entire life, she had done everything she could to prove herself as a good member of the Amish community. She had been looking forward to her baptism the next fall so that she could finally be an official member of the church.

"What's ailing you?" her mamm asked. "That's the third time I've caught you daydreaming today, daughter."

Priscilla shook her head, dismissing any thoughts of the bishop and Susie Byler. "I'm sorry, Mamm. Just a lot on my mind."

"You still thinking about that girl?" Mamm asked, eyeing Priscilla.

Her shoulders fell and the tears began to well up in her eyes. "I'm so worried, Mamm."

Her mamm frowned, her lips pressed together in a tight line. "I see," she said. "Why don't you sit down? I'll make you a nice cup of tea and we can talk, ja? Sometimes a little talking can make everything a lot better."

Priscilla collected her thoughts as she sat at the long table, waiting for her mamm to join her. She needed those few minutes to grasp what, exactly, was bothering her the most. She had spoken the truth: she was worried. She just didn't know what to expect from Susie's complaint to the bishop.

64

Setting the cup of tea before her daughter, Mamm sat down at the chair that was normally reserved for Daed. She smoothed some crumbs from the top of the tablecloth and looked over at her daughter. "What's eating at you, Priscilla?"

"Oh Mamm," Priscilla started, the tears now falling freely down her cheeks. "I just don't understand how this girl can make up such lies! How can she call herself a follower of Christ if she can act so unchristian?"

Mamm sighed. "I thought that might be the problem."

"I don't understand why she is constantly picking on me," Priscilla said, wiping at her tears. "I didn't provoke her, I hardly even knew her. She just keeps looking for ways to make me look bad or hurt my standing within the community."

"She is doing that, indeed," Mamm nodded.

Priscilla continued. "And I'm worried about Stephen. He works so hard and has such a good reputation. I don't want her damaging him or, even worse, forcing him to choose between his image as a good Amish man and his feelings for me."

"That could happen, ja" Mamm said softly.

"And the bishop!" Priscilla said. "I am hurt that he just accepted Susie Byler's accusation at face value without investigating further. I've been a part of this community far longer than she has. I have never done anything harmful to anyone. It hurt me that he was so quick to reprimand me without considering other angles."

"I can see where that would be hurtful," Mamm agreed.

Priscilla frowned and looked at her mother. It dawned on her that her mamm had been merely listening to her but not offering any advice. "What should I do?"

"What can you do, daughter? You can't control any of

these situations, now, can you?" her mamm asked softly. "Don't you believe that God will watch over you? Perhaps this is a test of your faith in Him."

"A test?" Priscilla asked, her eyes opening wide. She had never thought of it that way.

"Ja, a test," Mamm replied. "You can't change the outcome of any of these situations. But you can believe in God and that He knows what He is doing. I have always believed that there is a reason for everything. Sometimes situations don't seem to present those reasons right up front." She hesitated, her finger tracing an imaginary line on the tabletop. "I don't speak of this much but you know that I lost a baby before you and Jonas were born."

This was news, indeed. "Oh Mamm! I never knew!"

Mamm shrugged. "Ja, was a stillborn," she said. Her eyes seemed to darken as she traveled back in time to that terrible day. "I was so upset. Just devastated, as you can imagine. Your daed was right gut to me but it took me time to get past the fact that God would take one of my precious babies."

"I'm so sorry," Priscilla whispered.

Mamm lifted her eyes and stared at Priscilla. "You shouldn't be," she said sternly.

The tone of her voice startled Priscilla and she jumped at the words. "Whatever do you mean?"

"Think about it, Priscilla," her mamm said. "If that baby had lived, I wouldn't have had Jonas and most likely you would not have been born. I might have had other babies but they would have been different babies, not my Jonas and my Priscilla!" Mamm smiled softly. "I often think that God took that baby so that I could have you and your brother. It was a hard sacrifice but, like Abraham with Isaac, who are we to question God?"

A light dawned within Priscilla. She began to understand what her mamm was saying. "Good can come out of evil," she whispered.

Mamm took a deep breath. "I'd like to think so," she said. She smiled at her daughter. "And I would add that Susie Byler and her jealous accusations will eventually backfire on her. No one can live with the burden of such lies and hatred without being found out, Priscilla. Trust your mamm on that one." She reached over and placed her hand over Priscilla's. "And know that your daed and I are very proud of you and how you have conducted yourself during these ordeals."

"*Danke*, Mamm," Priscilla said. "That means a lot to me."

"And I suspect that you have nothing to fear with that Stephen Esh," her mamm added. "He's a gut man with his intentions set on one thing." She paused and stared at her daughter. "You."

For a moment, neither spoke. Priscilla was thinking about what her mamm had said. Deep down, she knew that Stephen seemed serious about her and had made it clear that he was willing to wait for her. But she had been totally unaware that so many other people knew about his intentions. Usually courting was kept private. Clearly, with Stephen being so much older and established, there were many eyes watching him to see where his heart would land. And it appeared to have landed in her hands.

"Now," Mamm said, breaking the awkward moment of silence, "We need to start preparing for Saturday. The women will be coming over for quilting, ja? And we certainly cannot have the house looking like we don't clean it, now, can we?" She stood up and glanced around the room. "And with Elsie's *kinner* coming over on Friday, we will need to keep them outside so that they don't mess up the kitchen even more than usual!"

Priscilla didn't have to ask what needed to be done. Instead, she set to work to make certain that the floorboards were clean and the furniture dusted. She enjoyed working alongside her mamm in the house. Cleaning was one of her favorite chores because the house sparkled when they were finished and it smelled wunderbaar gut! Even more importantly, she knew that the time she spent with her mamm was special. She was learning how to care for the home, something she'd be doing for her own family someday. And, according to her mamm, that day might actually be much sooner than she had anticipated.

It was a thought that warmed her on the inside and put a smile on her face as she worked her way around the house.

Chapter Ten

It was Saturday morning and Priscilla stared at the quilt stretched over the large wooden frame. It was truly a beautiful quilt and the pattern was rather different. She knew that it would take several more gatherings before the quilt top was completed. She imagined that it would be finished by the end of January, if the weather was good. By February, they would be focusing on binding the edges. Then, it would be folded up and packed away in her hope chest. Just in time for the beginning of field preparations for spring plowing, seeding and planting, she realized.

When the women arrived, Priscilla greeted each one enthusiastically while Mamm took their wraps. The day was chilly and many of the older women had worn their black capes over their dresses. There had been an early snow and several inches covered the ground. But it was unusual to get snow so early in the winter. Priscilla wondered if they would have a white Christmas this year.

By ten-thirty, there were eight women seated around the quilting frame, needles in their fingers and thread on their laps. Priscilla sat between her mamm and Lizzie, listening to the women share their family stories and some community gossip. She loved to hear their laughter and listen to their casual banter. Usually at church, the conversation was more reserved and formal. There also a lot of work to do in serving all of the congregants so there wasn't as much time for socializing. So the quilting bee was a wonderful time to get caught up and share with each other in a less formal fashion.

"I heard the Byler's are having their own quilting bee,"

Lydia mentioned, her eyes shifting over to Priscilla's for just a split second. When Priscilla looked up, Lydia averted her eyes. "Seems Jacob's daughter is preparing her own wedding quilt."

Lizzie scoffed. "Going to be in her hope chest for quite a while, if she keeps acting up the way she does."

An older woman named Mildred gasped, "Lizzie Miller!"

Lizzie frowned and lifted up her tired blue eyes, staring across the quilt at Mildred. "It's true and we all know about it. There's a firefly in the room and no one is recognizing it. Instead, we're just chasing it!" Lizzie paused long enough to turn her gaze around the room. "We all know what she has been saying about Priscilla. It's time the community did something about it." She lowered her head back to the quilt. "That child needs some help and if we don't help her, who will then?"

"Her parents aren't helping, that's for sure and certain" Lydia added under her breath.

Mamm clucked her tongue. "I would rather not hear such talk over my daughter's wedding quilt. Brings bad luck!"

Lizzie waved her hand at Mamm dismissively. "Bad luck is that girl saying that Priscilla's quilt was a stolen pattern." There was a collective silence among the women as if they were all holding their breath. "I've seen this pattern before. I happen to know that it's uncommon because of how complicated it is. But it's a pattern that has graced many beds throughout the years. Claiming to steal a pattern! Such nonsense!"

"Lizzie," Mamm said softly, an unspoken warning in her voice.

Priscilla lowered her eyes, her heart pounding inside of

her chest. On the one hand, she was glad that people were defending her. Yet she still felt horrible for Susie Byler. Now that people in the community knew what Susie was saying, her reputation was truly soiled and it would, indeed, be hard for her to find a marital bed to cover with her own wedding quilt.

"Perhaps we should sing?" Priscilla offered quietly. She glanced around the quilting frame at the other women and, with relief, noticed that several were nodding their heads. They, too, were eager to move onto a different subject. It seemed that Susie Byler was a topic that no one really wanted to discuss.

"You pick a song from the Ausbund, Priscilla," Lizzie invited, resting her weathered hand atop Priscilla's. "It's your quilting and I want to hear your lovely voice."

Everyone nodded eagerly in agreement. Quickly, Priscilla thought for a moment, trying to think of a hymn that could change the tone of the quilting back to fellowship and joy. A smile crossed her lips as Song 95 came to her mind. With a soft voice, she began to sing the first line and the other women joined in as they sung:

> With pleasure and joy I will sing praises to God,
> Unto the Father good,
> My Spirit does strive thereafter,
> For He my heart does gladden,
> And with His grace stands by me always.
>
> O Lord God, You have chosen me through grace
> On this earth
> And numbered me among Your children.
> Therefore Your name is praised,
> All my life I give thanks to You.
>
> Your glory I cannot magnify enough,
> That You will not

Hold me accountable for sin anymore,
You take me on as Your child,
For this I thank You with a heartfelt desire. [2]

When the group of women had stopped singing, Priscilla looked around at their faces. There was a feeling of peace about the room as the words from the Ausbund hymn reverberated in the silence. It was as if the surrounding walls had captured the essence of the hymn and had everyone present basking in its comforting outreach. Mamm looked over at Priscilla and, despite her attempts to hide it, she was clearly proud of her daughter. Her face glowed and there was a hint of tears at the corners of her eyes.

"Lovely choice," Lydia finally said, her voice catching in her throat.

Priscilla flushed and turned her attention back to the quilt. Her song had worked to change the tone of the quilting bee. The women began to share stories again and there was no more talk about the quilt pattern or Susie Byler. Instead, the focus was on family stories about children and grandchildren, crops and cows. She took a deep breath, pleased in the way the conversation had shifted.

It was noon when the younger girls showed up. Priscilla noticed that it was only Polly, Sarah, and Anna who arrived to help with the quilt. She was glad to see her friends but disappointed that none of the other young girls had arrived. She greeted her three friends and glanced back at the older women who were still bent over the quilting frame.

"I suspect no one else is coming?" she whispered.

Polly shook her head. "They are all believing Susie," she

---

[2] Ausbund, Song 95, verse 1-3.

admitted. "I don't understand the hold that she has over these people."

With a sigh, Priscilla tried to smile. "I'd rather have three true friends beside me than ten false ones." The words sounded nice and she did believe it. Yet, it stung that other young women that she had considered friends had turned their backs on her.

Sarah gave her a quick hug. "It will all be fine," Sarah said as she pulled back. "People will soon learn the truth about Susie Byler."

Anna raised an eyebrow. "Mayhaps sooner than you think. I overheard my daed talking to the bishop," she said. Priscilla always forgot that Anna's uncle was the bishop of their district. "He's none too happy about any of this. Says it's dividing the community."

Polly nodded. "That it is."

Sarah shook her head. "She just needs to leave you alone, Priscilla. I don't know why she has such a bee in her bonnet toward you."

Before Priscilla could answer, Polly responded with a hand wave and rolling of her eyes. "Oh, please! Of course we know why! Susie is just outrageously jealous of Priscilla. The more Priscilla ignores Susie's antics, the more infuriated Susie becomes. It will be her downfall."

"Like Haman," Anna said.

The other girls nodded in agreement. "Like Haman," Polly affirmed. "Now, let's have no more talk of that wicked girl and let's enjoy this quilting bee. That's why we are here, ain't so? Let's not empower Susie Byler with our thoughts and conversation but enjoy each other's company."

Priscilla smiled, feeling better already. "Now that is something I can agree with!"

Despite the fact that there were so few young women attending the quilting bee that day, Priscilla thought it was the most special day. Her good friends had showed up, demonstrating their support for Priscilla. Polly's wisdom was well put. Priscilla would not empower Susie Byler anymore.

Chapter Eleven

For the next week, Priscilla helped her Mamm at home. The upcoming church Sunday was to be held at their house and Mamm insisted that every piece of furniture be moved so that the floors were scrubbed by hand and baseboards oiled so that they shone. Despite having cleaned the house the week before, Priscilla didn't complain. She knew how her mamm felt about having a spotless house.

"Cleanliness is next to godliness," she would always say.

By Thursday, Mamm insisted that Jonas and David move the quilting frame out of the gathering room. Carefully, they disassembled what they could and moved it into the downstairs master bedroom. In order to get it into the room, the bed had to be disassembled. It was a major production and Priscilla felt pangs of guilt that so much trouble had to be made on behalf of her quilt.

"Don't be silly," Jonas said as he and David leaned the mattress against the wall. "It's not a bother."

"It sure looks like a bother," she replied as she leaned against the doorframe.

David scowled. "For anyone else, it *would* be a bother."

Jonas laughed.

On Friday and Saturday, Priscilla spent the day baking bread and chopping vegetables for the salads that would be served. They made fresh butter and cup cheese, too, a favorite among the Amish. By Saturday night, they were both exhausted and looking forward to the following day, knowing that they wouldn't have to host the Sunday service again until the following Spring.

When she awoke on Sunday morning, it was five o'clock. She quickly dressed and pinned back her hair, careful to place her black prayer kapp, reserved for unmarried young Amish women, upon her head. Looking in the small mirror, she pinched her cheeks, hoping to get some color to her pale skin. She missed the summer months and having a healthy glow to her skin: One of the many downsides to winter, she thought.

It was just slightly after eight o'clock when the first people began to arrive. Black capes and bonnets were set aside in the canning room and snowy shoes were stomped against the floor. Despite their caution, small puddles of melted snow quickly covered the floor. Jonas and David made certain to wipe up the water so that no one would slip.

Priscilla stood tall, next to her mamm as the women greeted them with a handshake and a kiss. It was usually the older women who arrived first, either with their husbands or with a neighbor if they were widowed. Quite a few among them had been at the Smucker house the week before for the quilting and Priscilla found that she felt closer to these women than she ever had, before the quilting bee had started.

The clock ticked closer to nine and the younger Amish women began to arrive with their children. Priscilla loved to see the children on Sundays. Most Amish mothers dressed their children in the same color dresses and shirts. That made it easier to identify which child belonged to which mamm.

When the Esh family arrived, Stephen's mamm greeted Priscilla with a warm smile. "I hear you have quite a quilt being made," she whispered into Priscilla's ear. "I intend to stop by next Saturday for some quilting as well, if that suits you."

Priscilla flushed, realizing that she had never really spoken to Stephen's mamm before and, if he had it his way, she would one day be her mamm, too. "That suits just fine," she said softly.

As Stephen's mamm continued down the line, greeting the other women, Priscilla looked up and felt her heart sink into her chest. She hadn't thought about the Byler family showing up but there, at the end of the line, was Susie and her mamm. For the past few Sundays, Priscilla had avoided greeting Susie. Now, as the host family, there was no getting around it. She would have to shake Susie Byler's hand and greet her with a kiss.

Judas' kiss, she thought bitterly. How could she possibly extend a hand in fellowship to this woman who continued to delight in causing so much trouble for her? She felt her pulse quicken and she reached out for her mamm's hand. Squeezing it, she leaned over and softly said, "Please don't make me do this."

Mamm squeezed her hand back but said nothing in reply.

Taking a deep breath, Priscilla glanced around the room and noticed that most eyes were turned in her direction. If she turned to leave, everyone would notice. She swallowed, feeling her throat constrict and her heart race even faster. The color drained from her face and she pressed her lips together, knowing that she had no choice. She straightened her back and took a deep breath as the Bylers approached.

"*Gude Mariye,*" she said as Susie's mamm stood before her. Priscilla leaned forward and kissed Susie's mamm as she shook her hand. There was no response.

Susie stood beside her own mamm, her eyes narrow and piercing as she waited to greet Priscilla. The room was silent. Priscilla lifted her chin and held out her hand toward Susie. But Susie merely glanced down at the outstretched hand then lifted up her eyes to stare into Priscilla's face. With no further reaction, Susie turned on her heels and continued down the line, Priscilla's hand left in the air.

Priscilla felt her cheeks burn and she glanced at her mamm but Mamm was already greeting the next person. As Priscilla looked around the room, she noticed that everyone quickly averted their eyes, everyone except for the steely blue eyes of the bishop who stood in the doorway. He had witnessed the scene. His jaw was clenched tight and she thought she saw a flash of anger in his expression. But, just as quickly as she thought she saw it, it disappeared.

She felt a tug on her arm. Glancing over, she saw her mamm gesture toward the gathering room. It was time to single file into the room. Since they were the host family, Priscilla would not enter with the other young, unmarried women but with her mamm. The elderly women would enter first, the oldest women in the district leading the line. The older women sat in more comfortable chairs while the rest of the women would sit on the hard benches. After the women sat, the men would enter. The married men would follow the elderly men. The last to enter were the unmarried men.

Once everyone was situated, the men removed their hats and placed them under their seats. One man began to sing the first word of a hymn, his baritone voice deep and strong. It reverberated throughout the room before the rest of the congregants joined in, singing the rest of the line of the hymn in a long, drawn out manner. Each line of the hymn began the same way, with the lone baritone voice starting before everyone else joined in.

Priscilla forgot about Susie Byler who was seated two rows behind her among the other unmarried women. Instead, Priscilla found herself lost in the song, listening to the words.

> *Where shall I turn to,*
> *I, the least of the brethren?*
> *Alone to God my Lord,*
> *Who will be my helper.*
> *In all my needs,*
> *I trust in you, o God!*
> *You will not forsake me,*
> *And will stand by me until death.*
>
> *I have chosen for myself,*
> *My God, Your precious Word,*
> *Therefore have I lost*
> *The world's favor in all areas.*
> *God's favor I love more,*
> *Therefore I left the world.*
> *Take leave, wicked world,*
> *I'll stay on Christ's pathway.* [3]

When the singing was over, the congregation sat quietly, waiting for Bishop Zook and the ministers to enter. They were last to enter, having stayed behind to discuss who would preach the sermon. It was always decided at the last minute, left up to God to guide them as to what was to be shared among the people.

As the ministers took their seats, the bishop remained standing. Clearly, he was the one that was selected to speak today but he took his time to begin. In the silence, he stood before the gathering, his hands behind his back as he paced

---

[3] Ausbund Song 76, verse 1-2.

back and forth. For a long time, longer than normal, he remained silent. People started to shift on the benches and a few of the younger people whispered to each other, wondering what was taking the bishop so long to begin.

"There is an evil among us," he began, his voice strong and clear. The congregation sat up straight and listened. It was unusual for the bishop to be so straight-forward with his sermon. "An evil, I tell you. And we must speak about this evil to combat it."

He leveled his eye at the many staring back at him. He gazed around the room. "'I trust in you, o God!' is the words of our opening hymn today. How many of you trust in God?" He paused. "Or do you instead pretend to trust in God?" He turned and stared at the women. "The hymn continues with 'You have deceived me long enough and detrained me with your multitude.' And I say that there is enough deception among our people. A deception that has been distracting the community from God's favor."

His eyes stopped and stared at Susie Byler. "I, too, have been deceived and found myself the 'servant of sin'. No more!" He raised his voice. "I repeat. No more!"

He turned away and stared at the wall, his back to the people. "There has been too much gossip among the people. It must stop." Whirling around, he raised his hand over his head. "I will hear no more about this nonsense of stealing quilt patterns," the bishop said, his voice loud and sharp. His eyes rolled across the heads of those gathered in the room for worship. "Quilt patterns do not belong to a person. Not in this community," he added. "It is a way for our women to express their creativity. Often these patterns are passed down through the generations. No one owns them." His words were piercing and loud. "No one."

There was a soft murmuring among the fellowship and several people looked at Priscilla while others glanced at Susie who hung her head, refusing to meet anyone's gaze. Priscilla didn't have to turn around to know what was happening behind her. She could sense the flames of embarrassment that consumed Susie's face. Beside her, she felt her mamm gently nudge her leg. But she didn't dare look at her.

"We are one people. We have a sense to God above all others. Clinging to such worldly possessions is not our way. We share in the glory and share in the defeat," he continued. "We. Are. One. People."

Priscilla kept her eyes on the bishop, feeling the heat of too many stares. She refused to look at the people. She knew that many of them were aware of what the bishop was saying and to whom he was speaking. She didn't feel vindicated by his speech. Instead, she felt a deep sorrow for Susie Byler. She could not imagine how Susie felt, hearing the bishop's public reprimand and knowing that the entire district was too aware that he was directing this sermon toward her.

For a moment, Priscilla felt tears at the corners of her eyes. Despite the horrible days she had experienced because of Susie Byler, Priscilla felt a deep sorrow for the young woman. It hadn't needed to be this way, she thought. If only Susie Byler hadn't been so jealous and spiteful, so full of lies and malcontent, perhaps they could have been friends.

"We are a community. A community focused on living a life that follows in the footsteps of our Savior. For someone to believe, we must remove ourselves from the temptation to speak ill of each other and to spread evil gossip about each other. We need each other and we need to support each other. That is what community is about, isn't it?" The bishop stopped pacing. "I will ask all of you to reflect about your own behavior. What have you done to contribute to well-being in the community? What have you done to make God pleased with us?"

There was silence among the congregation. The bishop stopped talking and stood there, his hands at his sides as he stared at the people. The silence continued. No one moved. It was a sobering moment. After all, the entire community had heard the words that were not just spoken to reprimand Susie Byler. Instead, they realized that everyone had permitted the gossip to continue throughout the past weeks. The reprimand was for everyone, those who had taken sides and those who had remained silent, permitting the split among the youth concerning the quilt to perpetuate.

The rest of the service continued as planned. The bishop sat down, another hymn was sung, then one of the ministers stood up to discuss a passage from the Bible. Priscilla tried not to look at the men that sat facing her on the other side of the room. She knew that Stephen Esh was there, probably watching her. She didn't want to meet his gaze. After all, he had also heard the sermon and probably knew that the discussion was about Susie Byler's gossip about the quilt and claims that Priscilla had stolen Stephen from her. She didn't want to face the embarrassment of seeing his expression. Surely he was just as mortified as she was about being associated with such a public reprimand. She wondered if he felt that his reputation was tarnished and the thought made her stomach twist. Even if they were not the cause of the problem nor had they provoked the bullying and gossip, they were at the center of it. Perhaps there was more that they should have done to prevent it.

After the end of service prayer, Priscilla hurried to help her mamm in the kitchen. She knew that it would be a long two hours as she was expected to work straight through, washing dishes and cups between the seatings. She was glad for the work. She didn't want to face the curious looks from the fellow worshippers. Nor did she want to bump into Susie Byler again.

The last family left at one-thirty and Priscilla took a deep breath. She had managed to stay busy and avoid too much conversation with any of the women. She also had avoided Stephen Esh, too afraid that he was upset with her for having caused unwanted attention on his character. She knew that she hadn't incited Susie but this was the second time that she had felt the wrath of Susie's bullying. Polly's words echoed in her ears from the quilting bee last week. Jealousy sure was an evil sin, she thought. Her only hope was that Susie would back off now that the bishop had spoken so publically about her poor behavior.

Chapter Twelve

She looked up when she heard the knock at the door. Church had ended hours ago and, with the deteriorating weather, no one was expected at the house for supper so the three short raps on the window of the door surprised her.

For the past hour, Priscilla had been sitting in the gathering room, her back to the kitchen as she stared at the window. The snow had been falling for a while, covering the fields in a heavy white blanket that looked so pure and heavenly. She had been staring at it, thinking that she wished she were a young girl and could go sleigh riding or make snow men in the field, anything to forget the horrible past few weeks.

"Priscilla?"

She raised her head and blinked as her eyes adjusted to the contrast of the brightness outside with the darkness in the house, for her mamm hadn't turned on the lamps yet. "Ja Mamm?" she answered.

"I think you have a visitor," Mamm said gently.

Scrambling to her feet, Priscilla ran her hands over the front of her dress and made certain her prayer *kapp* wasn't crooked before she hurried into the kitchen. Her daed was seated at the table, reading The Budget. There was a smile on his face but he didn't look up when Priscilla entered.

"Who's here, Mamm?"

Mamm gestured toward the utility room before turning back to the kitchen counter where she was preparing the food for the evening meal. She, too, had a soft smile on her face but said nothing.

Curious, Priscilla hurried toward the utility room. Her bare feet padded on the cold floor. Despite it being cold, she hated wearing shoes and dreaded the thought of the long winter with stockings and clunky black shoes that was ahead of her. Yet, this thought vanished from her mind as she walked through the door and saw Stephen standing at the center of the utility room.

"Stephen!" She started to smile then frowned. Was something wrong? "What are you doing here?"

He laughed. "That's some greeting, Priscilla!"

She shook her head and apologized quickly, "I'm sorry, I just meant if all was alright." After all, it was not very often that he had stopped by the house and always because of work related matters involving either her daed or her *brudder*. But that was the first time that he had asked to see her in person.

"Ja, ja," he said. "Was driving by and thought I'd poke my head in for a visit." He paused, glancing over her shoulder at the doorway to the kitchen. "Heard there was a pretty quilt getting made at your house. Wanted to see it for myself, if that's alright with you."

The color flooded to her cheeks. "You came to see the quilt?" she asked softly. After all of the trouble because of the quilt, she thought it would be the last thing anyone, especially Stephen, would want to see.

He lowered his voice. "Well, maybe I also wanted to see my girl," he added.

She heard footsteps behind her and turned to see her daed in the doorway. "You going to invite your guest in or let him freeze in that utility room, Priscilla?"

Flushing, Priscilla lowered her eyes and took a step

backward, making room for Stephen to enter. "I'm sorry," she whispered.

"What for?"

"Not inviting you in," she replied, feeling embarrassed that she hadn't thought to do so. She had been too stunned at seeing him standing there. Such a public arrival on her family's farm spoke volumes about his intentions.

He laughed. "Don't you worry about that, Priscilla. I wasn't really that cold anyway," he confessed in a soft voice as he brushed the snow from his shoulders.

"Gut __, Stephen," Mamm said when he entered the kitchen. She smiled at him, her eyes twinkling. "Mayhaps you'll be staying with us for supper then?" she asked.

He glanced at Priscilla and raised an eyebrow. "Reckon that would be right gut," he said. "I don't have to be back for evening milking. My brothers are both home tonight."

"You wanted to see the quilt?" she asked shyly.

He nodded and followed her through the kitchen toward the downstairs bedroom where the quilting frame had been set up.

She lit a lantern so that the room was basked in the glow of the light. There were shadows dancing on the walls but it illuminated the quilt, the colors bright against the white background. The pattern was even more beautiful in the light from the lantern, the blues and the greens of the boxes and squares popping out with all of the tiny stitches making a secondary pattern. The quilting pattern contrasted beautifully against the pattern of the hand-sewn patches.

As she stood there, staring at it, she sensed Stephen looking at it. She had never thought about asking him what he wanted in a quilt and quickly wondered if she should have conferred with him. But he put her at ease when he took a deep breath.

"Ja, vell," he said. "That sure is a beautiful pattern, Priscilla. I hope that it will grace a happy marriage bed one day."

"You like it?" she asked.

"Oh ja!" His voice was emphatically appreciative of the beauty contained in the quilt. "It shows creativity and love, not just from you but from all of the community. I think you have done a wonderful job selecting a pattern that is unique and traditional." He reached out and touched her hand, his fingers brushing her skin.

"I'm so glad," she whispered.

"And I'm hoping that it will be cherished for years to come," he added. "By both of us."

The color raced to her cheeks. She lowered her eyes, embarrassed by his candor. But she was also pleased to know that he was not upset about the sermon today. It dawned on her that was the very reason for his visit. Since there was no singing that night, he had come calling at her parents' farm to reassure her that he wasn't worried about having a soiled reputation or what people had been saying about her. She was still Stephen's Priscilla.

"I hope so, too," she replied and lifted her eyes to look at him.

She saw him glance over his shoulder at the door. Her mamm was still at the counter, preparing the food for supper and Daed's back was to them. Stephen squeezed Priscilla's hand and leaned over, gently brushing his lips against her cheek. When he pulled back, his eyes returned to the quilt, taking one last look at it. "It will," he said firmly. "Of that I'm sure and certain."

They returned to the kitchen. The meal was almost prepared and Priscilla hurried to help her mamm finish dishing the salads and applesauce into serving bowls. She hoped that the color had faded from her cheeks so that her mamm didn't ask her any questions later. But she still felt tingling on her skin where Stephen had kissed her.

"Where are David and Jonas?" she asked.

Daed looked up. "I believe I heard two buggies leave while I was finishing the milking," he said. "Must have been important. Jonas was sure driving awfully fast."

"Must be a lot of courting going on," Stephen said lightly. "I saw lots of fast moving buggies on the road tonight despite the snow."

"Was yours one of them?" Daed teased back.

"Daed!" Priscilla reprimanded.

Daed laughed. He gestured toward the table. "Come sit. Glad you were able to make it over tonight," he said. Priscilla raised an eyebrow, realizing that the visit by Stephen at her home might not have been entirely unplanned. Had her parents invited Stephen for supper? She was still wondering this as she heard her daed say, "I'm reading the Budget. Did you read about that farmer in Lititz? Found a skunk hibernating in his barn!"

Stephen laughed and sat down. "*Nee*. Can't say that I read that story." They began to discuss the skunk situation and then began talking about crops for the upcoming spring.

For a moment, Priscilla stood between the doorway and

the table. She watched as her daed and Stephen talked so naturally. They bantered back and forth like old friends. It warmed her heart to see that everything was back to normal. There was no discussion about the quilt, no discussion about the Susie Byler situation. Despite the cold, snowy weather outdoors, she felt a glow inside.

In that moment, she saw her future and she was happy. Following God and being a good Christian was more important than anything to her. But being surrounded by the love of her family was just as important. She counted the women of the community as part of that family. She had learned a lot from them during the past few weeks at the quilting bee and she suspected that she would learn a lot more in the upcoming weeks. But, for now, she was at peace with her life. God was blessing her with every gift that He gave her, as if her own life was a quilt with tiny stitches that represented His love.

She realized that the wedding quilt represented so much more than just a pretty pattern and fancy fabric. It represented the love of the community and the love of God. A married couple that slept beneath such a quilt was destined to be a happy one. And, as Priscilla stared at the young man who had made his intentions clear, she knew that her marriage would, indeed, be one of happiness and joy as long as Stephen was beside her.

Book Discussion Questions

By Pamela Jarrell, Administrator of The Whoopie Pie Book Club on Facebook

Question #1: Why do you think that Susie wouldn't leave things peaceful?

Question #2: Why do you think that Susie had such a hold on most of the younger girls? Do you think she was bullying them?

Question #3: What were Susie's ultimate motives for bullying Priscilla?

Question #4: In the first part of the story, Priscilla was hurt when she saw Susie in Stephen's buggy. Do you feel that she lacked confidence in Stephen's affection or was it just because she feared Susie's reputation?

Question #5: Should Priscilla's parents have approached Susie's parents to discuss the situation? Was it possible that Susie's mother was as devious as Susie was?

Question #6: Do you think that Bishop Zook handled the situation correctly?

Question #7: Is it better to ignore bullies, like Priscilla did with Susie, or is it best to confront them?

Love reading Amish romances and Amish Christian fiction? Please join the Whoopie Pie Book Club Group on Facebook where members share stories, photos, book reviews, and have weekly book club discussions.

ABOUT THE AUTHOR

The Preiss family emigrated from Europe in 1705, settling in Pennsylvania as the area's first wave of Mennonite families. Sarah Price has always respected and honored her ancestors through exploration and research about her family's history and their religion. At nineteen, she befriended an Amish family and lived on their farm throughout the years. Twenty-five years later, Sarah Price splits her time between her home outside of New York City and an Amish farm in Lancaster County, PA where she retreats to reflect, write, and reconnect with her Amish friends and Mennonite family.

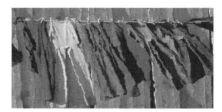

Find Sarah Price on Facebook and Goodreads!
Learn about upcoming books, sequels, series, and contests!

Contact the author at sarahprice.author@gmail.com.
Visit her weblog at http://sarahpriceauthor.wordpress.com or
on Facebook at www.facebook.com/fansofsarahprice.

Made in the USA
Charleston, SC
27 November 2012